Lifeboat Crew

by Nancy Dickmann

raintree

Raintree is an imprint of Capstone Global Library Limited, a company incorporated in England and Wales having its registered office at 264 Banbury Road, Oxford, OX2 7DY – Registered company number 6695582

www.raintree.co.uk
myorders@raintree.co.uk

Produced by Brown Bear Books Ltd:
Text: Nancy Dickmann
Design Manager: Keith Davis
Editorial Director: Lindsey Lowe
Children's Publisher: Anne O'Daly
Picture Manager: Sophie Mortimer
Printed and bound in India

ISBN: 978-1-4747-5546-7 (hardback)
21 20 19 18 17
10 9 8 7 6 5 3 2 1

ISBN: 978-1-4747-5550-4 (paperback)
22 21 20 19 18
10 9 8 7 6 5 3 2 1

British Library Cataloguing in Publication Data
A full catalogue record for this book is available from the British Library.

Acknowledgements
We would like to thank the following for permission to reproduce photographs:
Alamy: redsnapper, 11, 12, Robert Buchanan Taylor, 19; Getty Images: ARP/Oli Scarff, 6; iStock: oscarhill, 18; Maritime and Coastguard Agency: 9; RNLI: Nicholas Leach, 4, Looe, 15, Nigel Millard, 5 (bottom), 13, 14, 17, Cordelia Noble, 20, Andrew Parish, 16, Nick Sinclair, 21, Alan Stephen, 7, Wicklow, 1, Nathan Williams, 5 (top), 8; Shutterstock: Amazingmikael, 10, LRPS CPAGB/Philip Bird, cover

Brown Bear Books has made every attempt to contact copyright holders of material reproduced in this book. Any omissions will be rectified in subsequent printings if notice is given to the publisher. If anyone has any information please contact licensing@brownbearbooks.co.uk

Contents

Some words are shown in bold, **like this**. You can find out what they mean by looking in the glossary.

Call the lifeboat!

A lifeboat slides down a ramp, into the water. The **volunteer** crew are going to help people in trouble at sea.

Lifeboat crew help to save people in an **emergency**. They find and rescue people in difficulty in the water.

What lifeboat crew do

Lifeboats are ready for action 24 hours a day. They help people at sea, on rivers, lakes and during floods.

Flood rescue

Stormy sea

Lifeboat crew must be able to work in all weather conditions. They must be able to work in the dark and in storms. All crew are trained in **first aid**.

At the station

Most lifeboat stations are on the **coast**. Some have **slipways**. This means the lifeboat can be **launched** quickly.

Coastguards keep an eye on all activity in British coastal waters. When there is an **emergency** at sea the coastguard officer calls the lifeboat station. The lifeboat is ready and waiting.

Emergency call

Most lifeboat crew are **volunteers**. They have other jobs. They never know when they will get a call for help.

When a call comes, the crew rush to the lifeboat station. They get dressed and gather their **equipment**.

Lifeboat kit

Lifeboat crew wear special clothing to keep them warm and dry. They also wear boots and a safety helmet.

Life jacket

One of the most important pieces of kit is a **life jacket**. It keeps the crew member afloat in the water.

Lifeboats

Lifeboats must be fast, to reach people quickly. They are also strong. Some can flip themselves up again if they **capsize**.

Smaller **inflatable** lifeboats operate near the shore or in rivers. They rescue people from the water. Bigger lifeboats go further out to sea.

Saving lives

Many lifeboats have lights to help the crew spot people in the water. Lifeboats can pull other boats to safety if they are damaged.

Lifeboats carry medical **equipment**. The crew look after injured people. They give **first aid** until other medical help arrives.

Lifeguards

Lifeguards and lifeboat crews often work together. Lifeguards **patrol** many beaches. They rescue swimmers who need help.

Rescue tube

Jetski

Lifeguards use small boats and jetskis to rescue people. They carry **rescue tubes**, ropes and **life jackets**. If more help is needed the lifeguards call the lifeboat station.

Teaching the public

Lifeboat crew and lifeguards sometimes visit schools. They talk to children about their jobs and explain how people can stay safe in the water.

You can visit many lifeboat stations. The lifeboat crew will show you the lifeboat. They will tell you about the **equipment** and special clothing.

Staying safe

Beach safety:

- Only swim at beaches with lifeguards.
- Never go in the water if the red flag is up. A red flag means danger.
- A red-and-yellow flag tells you that a beach is safe.
- Never go into the water on your own.
- If you need help, raise your hand and shout.
- If you see someone in trouble call 999 and ask for the coastguard.

Danger! No Swimming

Swimming area with lifeguards

Glossary

capsize flip over in the water

coast the land next to the sea

coastguard organisation that patrols and protects a nation's coasts

emergency serious situation, such as a fire or boat accident, that calls for fast action

equipment items that a person needs to do their job

first aid emergency medical help given while waiting for a doctor

inflatable small rubber or plastic boat filled with air

launched rolled into the water

lifeguard expert swimmer who keeps watch on people in the water

life jacket sleeveless jacket that keeps a person afloat in the water

patrol guard an area by making regular walks through it

rescue tube foam-filled float carried by lifeguards

slipway a slope or ramp used for launching boats into the water

volunteer person who does a job without being paid

Find out more

Books

Call the Coastguard (In an Emergency), Cath Senker (Franklin Watts, 2013)

Lifeboat Crew Member (Here to Help), Rachel Blount (Franklin Watts, 2016)

Lifeboat Crew Member (People Who Help Us), Rebecca Hunter (Tulip Books, 2014)

Websites

rnli.org/shorething

Go on a virtual tour of a real lifeboat

rnli.org/safety

Here are some useful tips on staying safe in and around water

rnli.org/what-we-do

Find out more about the RNLI (Royal National Lifeboat Institution)

Index